By Gregory Vogt

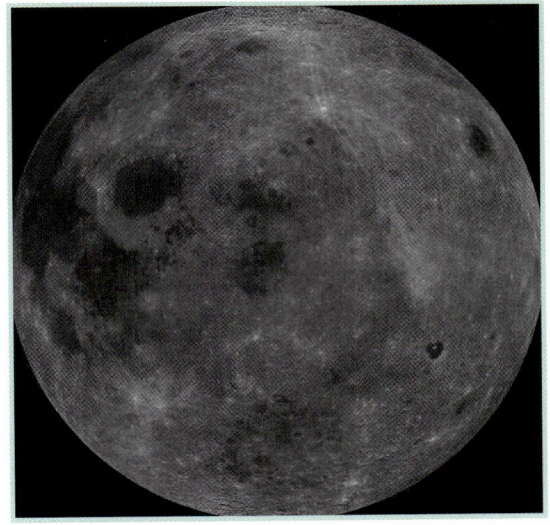

STECK-VAUGHN
ELEMENTARY · SECONDARY · ADULT · LIBRARY

A Harcourt Company

www.steck-vaughn.com

Copyright © 2001, Steck-Vaughn Company

ISBN 0-7398-3345-6

All rights reserved. No part of this book may be reproduced or utilized in any form or by any means, electronic or mechanical, including photocopying, recording, or by any information storage and retrieval system, without permission in writing from the publisher. Inquiries should be addressed to copyright permissions, Steck-Vaughn Company, P.O. Box 26015, Austin, TX 78755.

Printed and bound in the United States of America
1 2 3 4 5 6 7 8 9 W 04 03 02 01 00

Photo Acknowledgments
NASA/JPL, title page; NASA, cover, 10; NASA/USGS, 14; NASA, 16; NASA, 17; NASA, 18; NASA, 20; NASA/Malin Space Science Systems, 22; Dr. R. Albrecht, ESA/ESO Space Telescope European Coordinating Facility/NASA, 24; NASA/DLR, 26; NASA/DLR, 28; NASA/DLR, 30; NASA/DLR, 32; NASA, 35; NASA, 36; NASA, 39; NASA, 40; NASA, 42; NASA; 44

Contents

Diagram of the Moon 4

A Quick Look at Moons 5

Sixty-Eight Known Moons 7

Earth's Moon 11

Moons of Mars and Pluto 23

Moons of Jupiter and Saturn 27

The Outer Moons 41

Glossary 46

Internet Sites and Addresses 47

Index 48

Diagram of the Moon

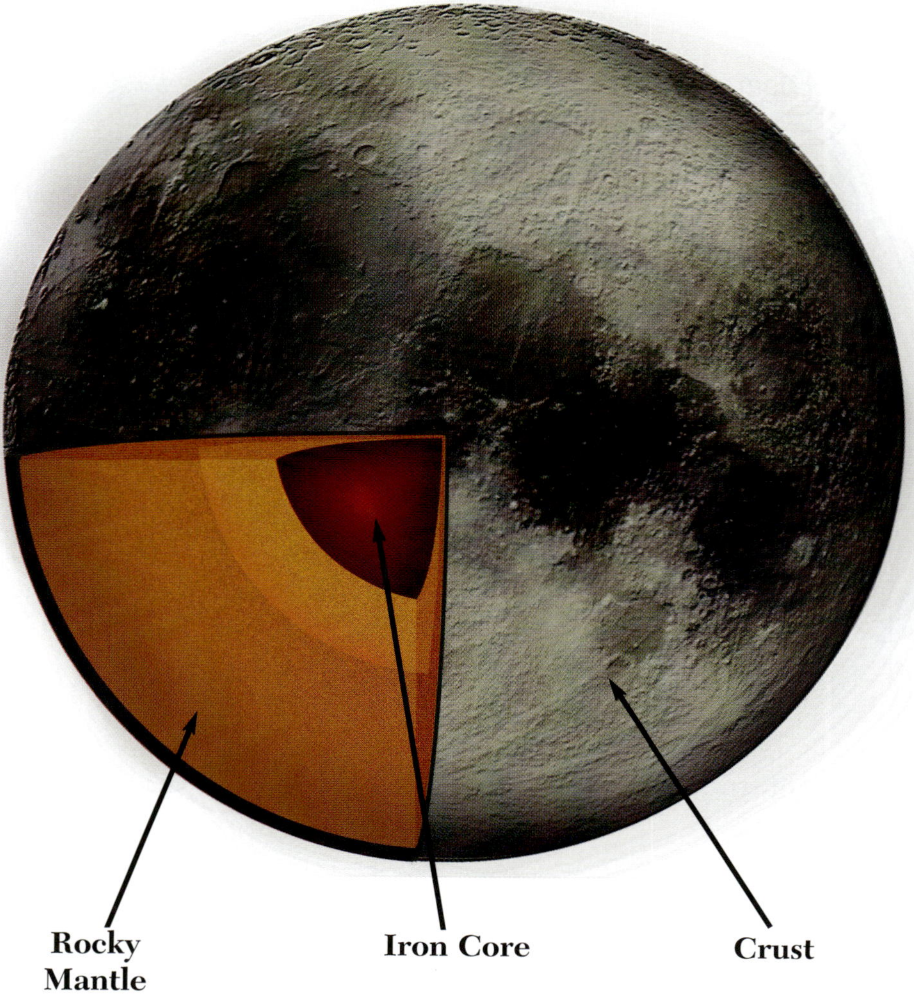

Rocky Mantle

Iron Core

Crust

A Quick Look at Moons
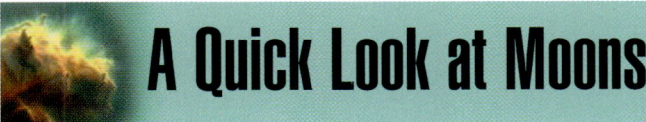

What are moons?
Moons are natural objects that circle around planets.

What are moons made of?
Moons are made of rock or rock and ice.

Do all planets have moons?
Mercury and Venus do not have moons. All other planets have one or more moons circling around them.

How many moons are there?
There are 68 known moons in the solar system.

Which planet has the most moons?
Uranus has the most moons. It has 21 known moons traveling around it.

What is the largest moon?
Jupiter's moon Ganymede is the largest moon in the solar system.

Sixty-Eight Known Moons

Earth's Moon is a large ball of rock and dust that circles Earth. It looks like a large white ball in the night sky. The Moon appears larger and brighter than all of the stars in the night sky. It is much closer to Earth than the stars.

Earth and the Moon are part of our solar system. The solar system is made up of the Sun and all the objects circling it. Our solar system has nine planets and 68 known moons. A moon is a natural satellite of a planet. A satellite is something that travels around something else.

Only two planets do not have moons. They are Mercury and Venus. Mercury is the closest planet to the Sun. Venus is the second planet from the Sun.

Astronomers may find more moons as they study the solar system. Astronomers are scientists who study objects in space.

Moons and Orbits

A moon is an object that travels around a planet. Moons are smaller than the planets they circle. Moons are usually large balls of rock or rock and ice.

Moons travel around planets in paths called orbits. Some moons have circle-shaped orbits. Other moons have orbits shaped like ovals. An oval is shaped like an egg.

A moon that orbits close to a planet travels very quickly. The planet's gravity pulls on the moon. This force is called a gravitational pull. Gravity is a natural force that attracts objects to each other. Massive objects have greater gravity. Massive objects contain a great deal of mass. Mass is the amount of matter an object contains. Matter is anything that has weight and takes up space.

Planets have greater gravitational pulls because they are more massive than moons. A close moon would crash into its planet if it traveled too slowly. Gravity gets weaker as a moon moves farther away from the planet. A distant moon travels more slowly.

Moons that are close to planets complete their orbits in just a few hours. Distant moons take much longer. One distant moon of the planet Uranus takes almost 1,300 Earth days to circle the planet once.

This diagram shows the different orbits of a planet's moons. The moon closest to the planet travels the fastest. The farther away a moon is, the slower it travels through space. The moon farthest away from the planet travels the slowest.

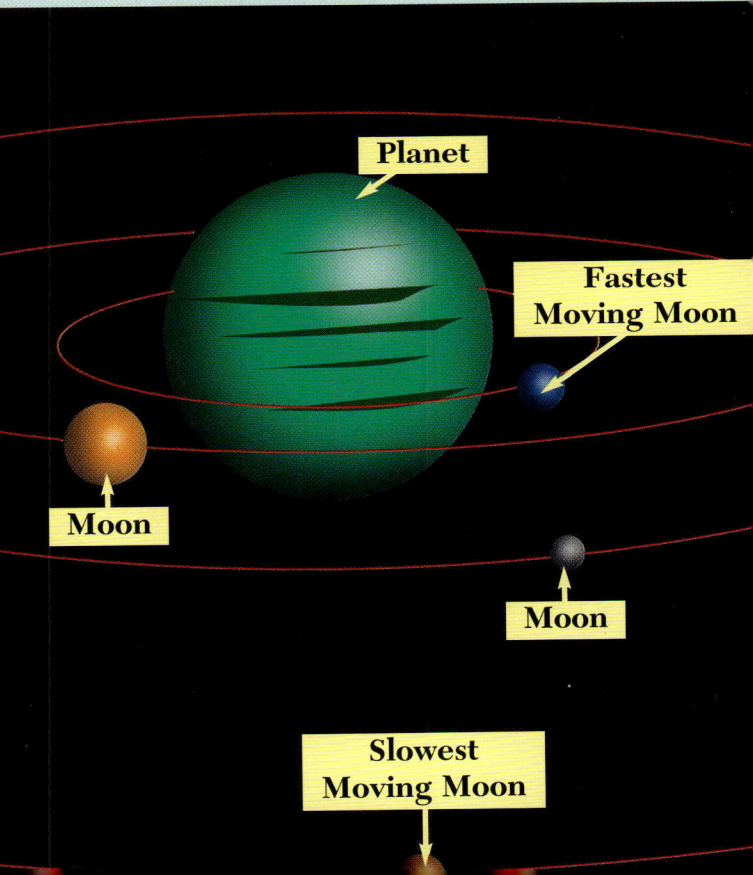

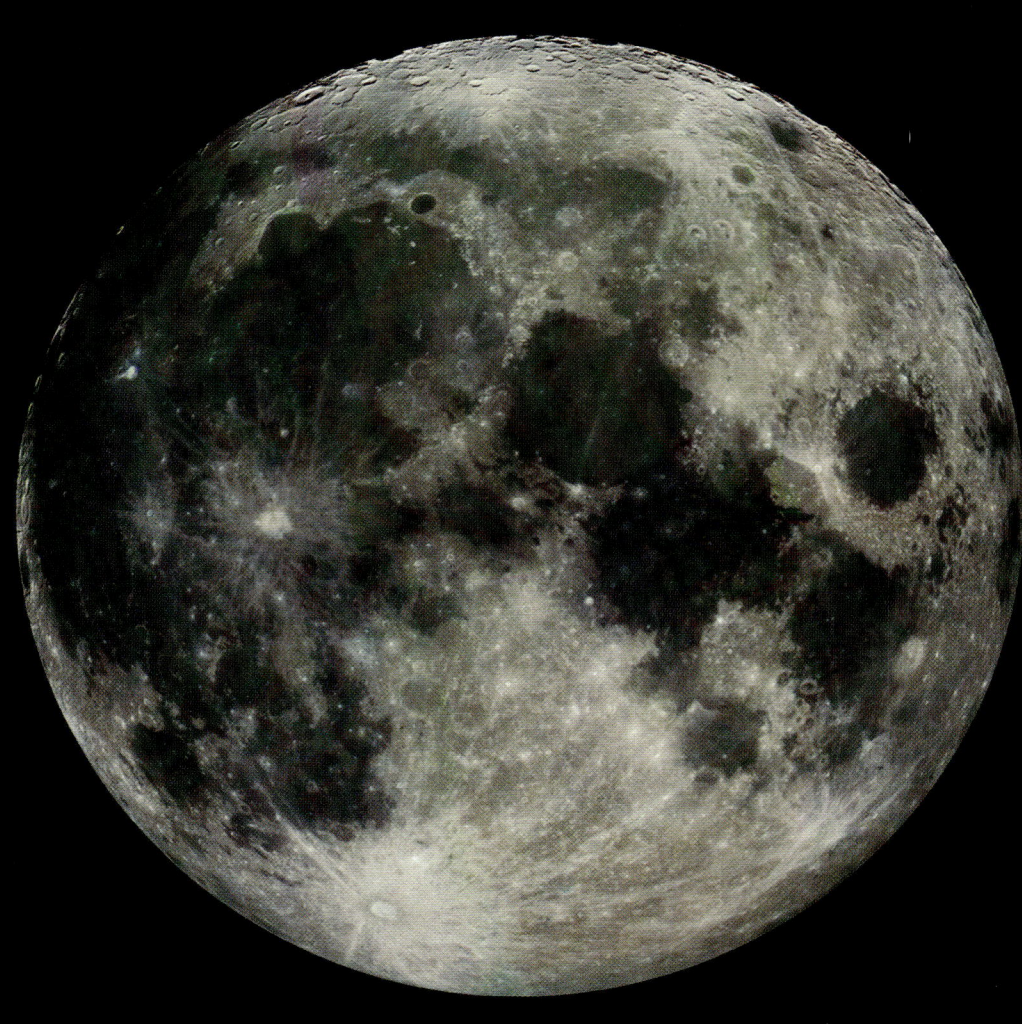

The *Galileo Orbiter* took this picture of the Moon. The dark areas are basins filled with lava rock.

Earth's Moon

The Moon is a rocky ball that is 2,159 miles (3,475 km) in diameter. It is an average of 238,600 miles (384,400 km) from Earth. The gravity of Earth keeps the Moon in orbit. The Moon circles Earth once every 29.5 days. The Moon turns as it orbits Earth. It spins around once every 29.5 days.

The Moon has a little gravity. The gravity of the Moon and the Sun pulls on the water in Earth's oceans. This makes the water rise and fall every day. Water gets deeper around the shores of the land. Then it flows back out to sea again. These regular changes in the water level are called the tides.

From Earth, the Moon looks black and white. It has light gray and black rocks on its surface. The light-colored areas of the Moon are mostly mountains and large craters. A crater is a large, bowl-shaped hole in the ground.

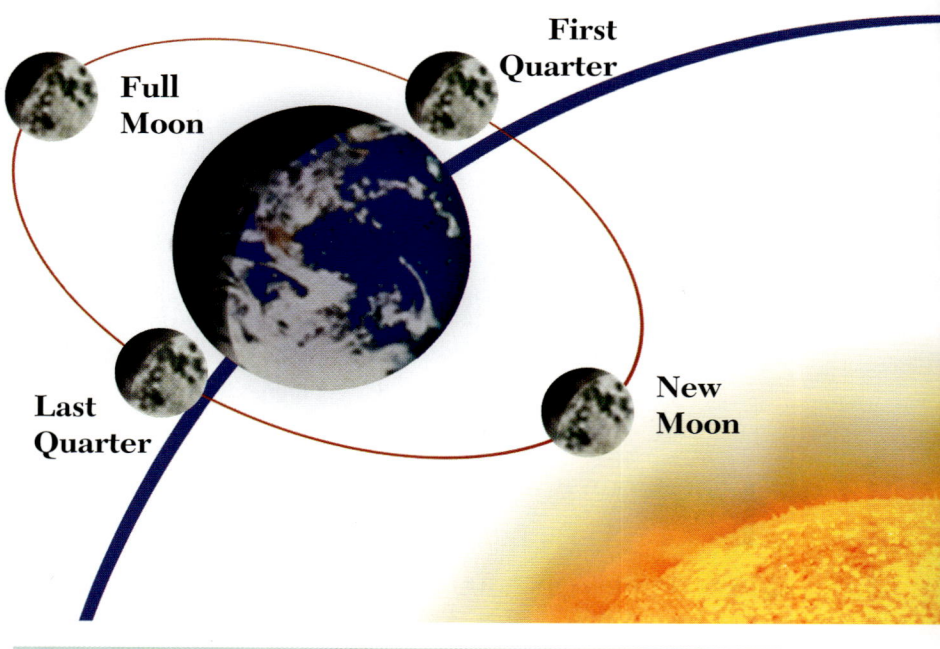

▲ This diagram shows how the changing positions of Earth and the Moon cause the Moon's phases.

Changing Moon

The Moon is very bright. But it does not give off any light of its own. Instead, it reflects light. The light shining from the Moon is really from the Sun. The sunlight bounces off the Moon and into space toward Earth.

The amount of sunlight that the Moon reflects back to Earth changes. At times, more sunlight is reflected toward Earth. When this happens, we see more of the Moon. The Moon falls into shadow at other times. Then less of its surface is lit up by the Sun. It reflects less light. This makes the Moon look different every night. The shape of the lit surface of the Moon changes. The different shapes are called the Moon's phases. It takes the Moon one month to complete its cycle of changing phases. Once the Moon's cycle is complete, it starts over again.

The Moon's orbit causes the phases. Sometimes the Moon is between Earth and the Sun. The Sun lights the side of the Moon facing it. At this time, the side of the Moon facing Earth appears dark. Other times, the Moon is on the other side of Earth. Then the lighted side of the Moon faces Earth.

Moon Calendar

New Moon

First Quarter
(seven days later)

Full Moon
(seven days later)

Last Quarter
(seven days later)

New Moon
(seven days later)

13

▲ A meteorite blasted the 58-mile (93-km) wide Copernicus Crater on the Moon's surface.

Meteorites

Small rocks and pieces of dust called meteoroids float in outer space. Meteoroids are called meteorites when they crash into other objects. Sometimes meteorites crash into the Moon. They cause explosions. The explosions blast some of the Moon's rock into space. This leaves craters in the surface of the Moon. Large meteorites blast huge craters. Small meteorites blast small craters.

The blasted rock rises into space and then falls back down to the Moon's surface. It piles up around the rim of the crater. Rays are what astronomers named the piles of blasted material around craters.

Very large meteorites make huge explosions on the Moon. This makes a huge crater. The explosion makes some of the rock inside the crater melt. The melted rock in the center of the new crater becomes smooth like the surface of a lake. When the rock cools, it forms a flat bottom.

Sometimes the melted rock in the middle of a big crater splashes upward. The rock cools before it falls back down. This creates a small mountain in the middle of the crater. Only large meteorites cause explosions hot enough to melt rock.

Ancient Surface

The surface of the Moon has not changed in billions of years. This is because the Moon has no wind, rain, or snow to wear away its surface. Craters on the Moon last billions of years. Earth has had many craters too, but most have been worn away.

Surface of the Moon

The surface of the Moon is made up of more than craters. It is covered with gray, dustlike soil. Mountains, craters, and smooth, flat places cover the Moon's surface.

Same Side

From Earth, you can only see one side of the Moon. It takes the Moon the same amount of time to turn once as it does to orbit Earth. To see the other side of the Moon, you have to travel in a spaceship. The *Galileo Orbiter* took this picture of the far side of the Moon.

The side of the Moon facing Earth has large smooth areas that are called maria. Maria are large basins that are completely filled with lava. Millions of years ago, melted rock called lava flowed from inside the Moon to the surface. The lava filled many large craters and basins. Lava turns into dark rock when it cools and hardens. The lava makes maria dark gray.

Light-gray craters surround maria. The Moon's craters are many sizes. The largest crater is 2,500 miles (4,023 km) across. The Moon's smallest craters are just large enough to hold a grain of sand.

The side of the Moon facing away from Earth has few maria. It is mostly covered with many large craters.

▲ Astronaut Edwin Aldrin became the second person to stand on the Moon during the *Apollo 11* mission.

Moon Walkers

Between 1962 and 1972, the National Aeronautic and Space Administration (NASA) ran the Apollo program. Each *Apollo* spacecraft had two parts. One part of the spacecraft was an orbiter that stayed in space. The other part was a lander that was built to land on the Moon.

There were six Apollo missions to the Moon. Rockets moved the spacecraft into space and toward the Moon. The trip to the Moon took three days.

Each spacecraft carried three astronauts. When they reached the Moon, one astronaut remained in the spacecraft. Two astronauts climbed into the lander. The lander had four legs and a rocket engine. The lander brought them down to the surface.

On the Moon, the astronauts wore spacesuits. The spacesuits gave them air to breathe and water to drink. The astronauts collected rocks and soil to bring home. They took many pictures of the Moon. They also set up experiments to learn about the Moon. One team of astronauts brought a special car to drive on the Moon.

The astronauts returned to the orbiter when they were finished exploring the Moon. Then the spacecraft rocketed back to Earth.

▲ Flowing lava cut this 60-mile (100-km) long channel. It is called the Hadley Rille. An astronaut took this photograph of the Hadley Rille on the Moon.

Where the Moon Came From

In total, the Apollo astronauts brought home 843 pounds (382 kg) of moon rocks. Scientists studied the moon rocks. They had many questions about the Moon that they wanted to answer.

Scientists wanted to find out the age of the Moon. They studied moon rocks and learned that it is more than 4.5 billion years old.

Scientists wanted to know what the Moon was made of. They discovered that moon rocks are made of many elements, such as the metals iron and titanium. Elements are pure materials found in nature. Moon rocks are much like lava rocks on Earth.

Scientists also wanted to know where the Moon came from. They are still not sure how the Moon formed. But some scientists think Earth was once struck by a huge meteorite. Most of the meteorite became part of Earth. But the explosion blasted pieces of the meteorite and Earth into space. Scientists believe that over millions of years, these pieces joined together and formed the Moon.

▲ *Mars Global Surveyor* took this close-up picture of the surface of Phobos in 1998.

 Moons of Mars and Pluto

The solar system has two main kinds of planets. Five planets are made of rock. The rocky planets are Mercury, Venus, Earth, Mars, and Pluto. Mars has the most moons of the rocky planets.

Mars has two moons called Phobos and Deimos. The two moons are shaped like giant potatoes. They each have many small craters on their rocky surfaces.

The moons are very small and are hard to see from Earth. Phobos is only 17 miles (27 km) in diameter. Diameter is the distance straight across a circle. Deimos is even smaller. It is only 9.3 miles (15 km) in diameter.

Phobos orbits 5,827 miles (9,378 km) above the surface of Mars. It circles the planet once every 7.6 hours. Deimos orbits 14,577 miles (23,459 km) above Mars. It circles the planet once every 28 hours.

The Hubble Space Telescope took the clearest picture of Pluto (left) and Charon (right) in 1994.

Pluto and Charon

Pluto was named after the Greek god of the dead. Pluto is a cold, dark place because it is the farthest planet from the Sun. Little sunlight reaches the surface of Pluto. It is 30 times farther from the Sun than Earth.

In 1978, U.S. astronomer James Christy found a moon orbiting Pluto. He named it Charon. In Greek stories, Charon was the boatman who brought people into the land of the dead.

Tiny Moon

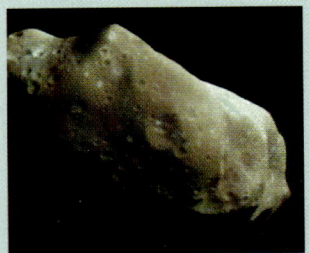

Even asteroids can have moons. A spacecraft on its way to Jupiter passed the asteroid Ida. The asteroid is 32 miles (52 km) long. Pictures sent back by the spacecraft showed that Ida has its own moon. A tiny chunk of space rock is orbiting it. The rock may have exploded from Ida when Ida was struck by a meteorite.

Charon is 737 miles (1,186 km) in diameter. That makes Charon half as big as Pluto. All other moons in the solar system are tiny compared to their planets. Astronomers call Pluto and Charon a double planet because of the closeness in size.

Charon orbits close to Pluto. It is only 12,179 miles (19,600 km) away from the planet. It takes Charon a little more than six days to orbit Pluto once.

Astronomers know very little about Charon because it is so far away from Earth. Astronomers believe hills of ice cover its surface. Charon may have a thin atmosphere. An atmosphere is a layer of gas surrounding an object in space. If there is an atmosphere on Charon, the gas most likely comes from Pluto.

NASA made this photograph from several photographs. It shows Jupiter and the four Galilean moons. The sizes and distances are not to scale.

Io

Europa

Ganymede

Callisto

Moons of Jupiter and Saturn

Four planets in our solar system are made mostly of gas. Like all planets, these giant planets orbit the Sun in a set order. Jupiter is the fifth planet from the Sun. It is followed by Saturn, Neptune, and Uranus. Most moons in our solar system orbit around these gas giants.

Jupiter is has 17 moons. Four of the moons are very large. These four moons are called Galilean moons. The famous astronomer Galileo discovered them in 1610. The other moons are tiny. In the 19th, 20th, and 21st centuries, astronomers discovered them with new, more powerful telescopes.

Astronomers found Jupiter's seventeenth moon in July 2000. It is the first Jupiter moon discovered in 21 years. It is also the smallest known satellite of a major planet. The moon has not been named yet.

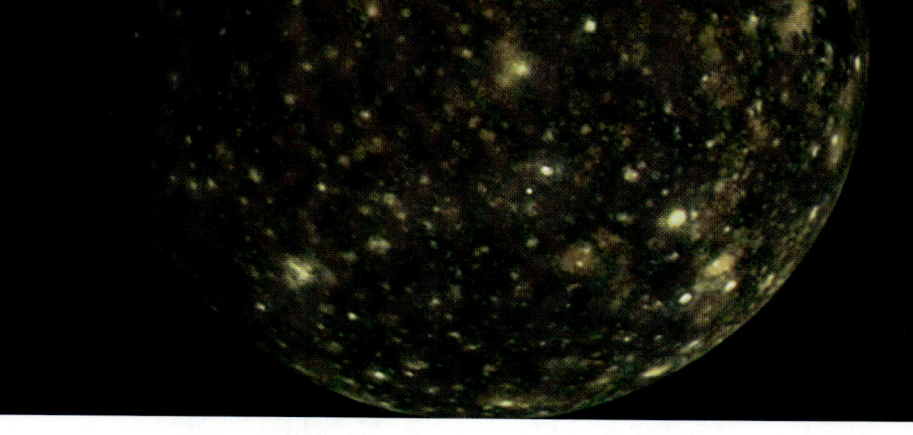

> The surface of Callisto has more craters than any place in the solar system.

Callisto

Of the Galilean moons, Callisto is the farthest away from Jupiter. Callisto orbits Jupiter at a distance of about 1.2 million miles (1.9 million km). This is about three times farther than Earth's Moon is from Earth.

Callisto is the third largest moon in the solar system. It is almost as big as the planet Mercury. Its dark surface is covered with dust-filled ice. Meteorite craters cover its whole surface.

Ganymede

Ganymede is the third farthest Galilean moon from Jupiter. It orbits Jupiter at a distance of about 620,000 miles (1 million km). Ganymede is the largest moon in the solar system. It is 3,273.5 miles (5,268 km) in diameter. This is larger than the planets Mercury and Pluto.

The United States sent the space probe *Voyager* to explore the solar system. A space probe is a spacecraft built to explore and gather information about space. In 1979, *Voyager* took pictures and recorded information about Ganymede. It sent this information back to scientists on Earth.

Pictures from *Voyager* showed that Ganymede has many craters. The craters tell astronomers that the surface of Ganymede is very old. Younger moons have very few craters. Ganymede is half rock and half ice. Its dark, icy surface is lined with cracks and grooves. Astronomers also think that Ganymede may have an ocean beneath its ice.

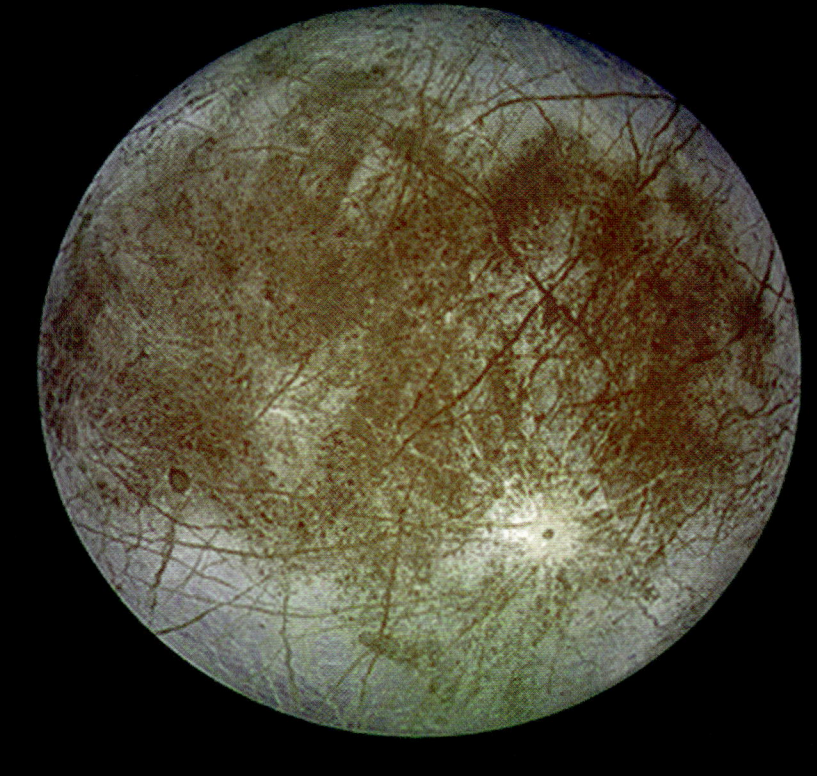

▲ **The *Galileo* spacecraft took this picture of Europa. It has many cracks in its smooth surface.**

Europa

Europa is Jupiter's second closest Galilean moon. It orbits at a distance of 416,900 miles (670,900 km) from the planet. Europa is the smallest of Jupiter's four Galilean moons. It is 1,945 miles (3,130 km) in diameter. This is a little smaller than Earth's Moon.

Europa is a bright moon. It reflects much of the sunlight that falls on it. A thin atmosphere surrounds Europa. The atmosphere has some oxygen, but not enough for people to live. People would have to bring their own oxygen to Europa to breathe.

Europa's surface is very smooth. It has very few craters. Only three craters on Europa's surface are larger than 3 miles (5 km) wide.

Miles of clear ice cover Europa's surface. Astronomers think Europa's ice may be floating on an ocean of water. Close-up pictures show many large grooves in the ice. There are also many cracks. Scientists think that the ice is broken into huge floating plates. If this is true, the markings are caused by huge ice plates drifting into each other. Europa's surface looks like a bunch of ice cubes that have frozen into one large block.

Any water under Europa's ice may be like Earth's oceans. If so, this the only other water ocean in the solar system that scientists have found so far. Some scientists think tiny forms of life may live in the water.

▲ **Io is the most volcanically active object in our solar system.**

Io

Io is the closest Galilean moon to Jupiter. It is 2,274 miles (3,660 km) in diameter. It takes only about 1.7 days to complete an orbit of Jupiter.

Voyager took pictures of Io and sent them back to Earth. Io is a rocky ball with a red, orange, and black surface. Some people compare the look of Io's surface to that of a huge cheese pizza.

Io is one of the few moons that has an atmosphere. Its atmosphere is mostly sulfur-dioxide gas. This gas is poisonous to people.

Many large, active volcanoes rise from Io's surface. These mountains form over cracks in the crust of a planet or moon. Ash, gas, and melted rock called lava sometimes erupt, or blow out, of volcano openings. Volcanoes on Io often erupt ash, lava, and sulfur. Sulfur is an element. Sulfur can be a solid, liquid, or gas. It can be red, yellow, or brown. The volcanoes also erupt huge clouds of sulfur-dioxide gas. Some of the erupted material falls back to the surface. Some volcanoes on Io are surrounded by huge, smooth lakes of lava.

Volcano eruptions blast some sulfur-dioxide gas into space. Some volcanoes explode columns of gas 250 miles (450 km) high. As Io orbits Jupiter, some of the gas leaves a sulfur-dioxide trail. This makes a circle-shaped cloud of sulfur-dioxide gas surrounding Jupiter.

Telescopes and Spacecraft

Astronomers send space probes into space to get a better view of Jupiter's moons. The *Voyager* and *Galileo* spacecrafts have each traveled to Jupiter. They took many close-up pictures of Jupiter and its moons. The pictures were sent back to Earth. *Galileo* stayed in orbit around Jupiter. The *Voyager* space probe went on to visit Saturn, Uranus, and Neptune.

Titan

Beyond Jupiter, the giant ringed planet Saturn orbits the Sun. Saturn has 18 named moons. Some astronomers think Saturn may have even more moons. Most of Saturn's known moons are only a few miles in diameter.

Titan is Saturn's largest moon. In fact, Titan is the second largest moon in the solar system.

Titan is one of the few moons in the solar system to have an atmosphere. Its atmosphere is thicker than Earth's atmosphere. It is made up mostly of nitrogen gas. Titan's atmosphere does not have much oxygen. People would need to bring oxygen to breathe on Titan.

Astronomers cannot see the surface of Titan. Its atmosphere is too cloudy and orange. An orange haze from the gases in its atmosphere surrounds the moon.

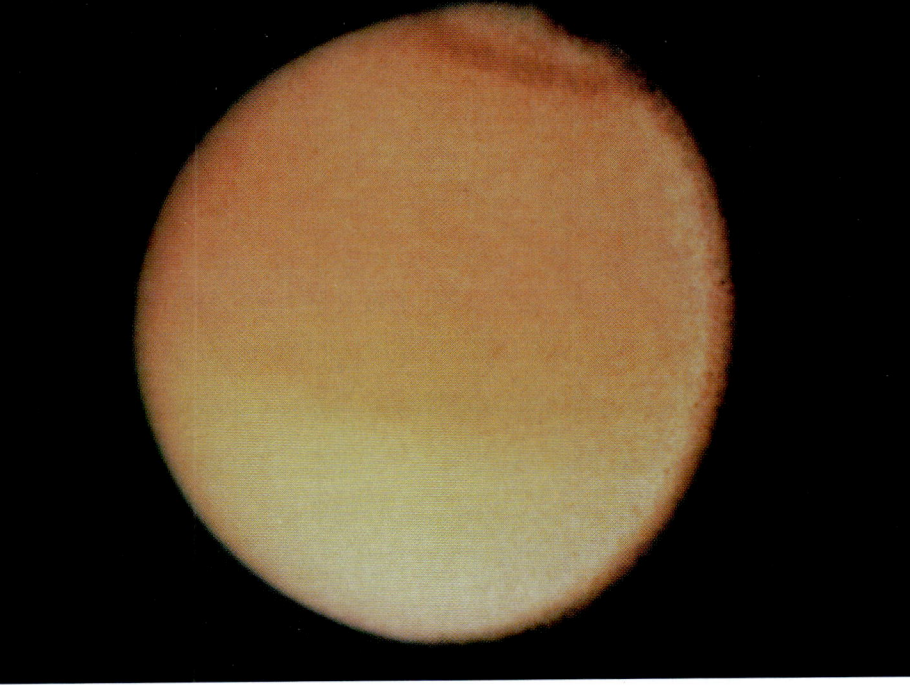

> ▲ **Scientists believe that Titan may have ethane-methane oceans on its surface.**

The temperature at Titan's surface is about –290° Fahrenheit (–178° C). This temperature is cold enough to turn some of Titan's gas into liquid form. Some astronomers think Titan may have a liquid-gas ocean.

Astronomers hope to learn more about the surface of Titan. They plan to send the *Huygens* space probe into Titan's atmosphere in 2004. The probe will examine the gases in the atmosphere. It will also take pictures of the surface of Titan.

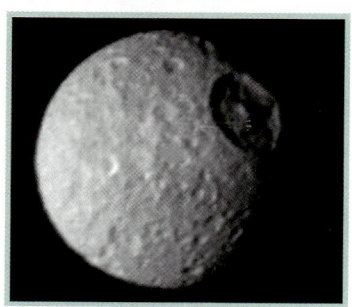

Mimas (top) was almost split in two by a large meteorite. The bottom photo shows the crater it made.

Mimas

Mimas is one of Saturn's smaller moons. It is 262 miles (421 km) in diameter. It orbits Saturn at a distance of 115,295 miles (185,540 km).

The surface of Mimas is marked with many craters. One of the craters is 81 miles (130 km) across. This is one-third the diameter of Mimas. It is the largest surface feature on the moon. In places, the crater is 6 miles (10 km) deep. This huge crater on Mimas was named Herschel Crater to honor the astronomer William Herschel. He discovered Mimas in 1789.

A great deal of heat was created when the huge meteorite hit Mimas and made the Herschel Crater. Heat from the explosion melted some of the rock. The melted rock splashed around the surface. Some of the rock splashed into the center of the crater. The rock cooled and formed a mountain. The mountain in the crater is more than 307 miles (494 km) high. This is more than 55 times higher than Mount Everest, the highest mountain on Earth.

Saturn's Rings

Moons are natural satellites of planets. But the gas planets also have rings. Rings are made up of millions of tiny rock and dust satellites. Most rings are small and difficult to see from Earth.

Saturn has wide rings circling it. To early astronomers, the rings made the planet look as if it had ears. With better telescopes, astronomers saw the rings more clearly. They counted several wide rings.

The *Voyager* space probe flew by Saturn. It took pictures of the rings. The pictures showed thousands of tiny rings. These rings formed into bands of rings. From Earth, the tiny rings together look like several big rings.

Saturn's rings are not solid bands. The rings are made of billions of rock particles. Each piece of rock is like a tiny moon orbiting the planet. The rock particles can be as small as pebbles or as big as houses. The particles are close together. They all move in the same direction as they orbit Saturn. This makes the rings look solid, but they are not.

The nearest rings are only a few thousand miles from the planet. The farthest rings are 87,000 miles (140,000 km) away from it.

▼ Saturn's rings are made up of many pieces of rock and ice.

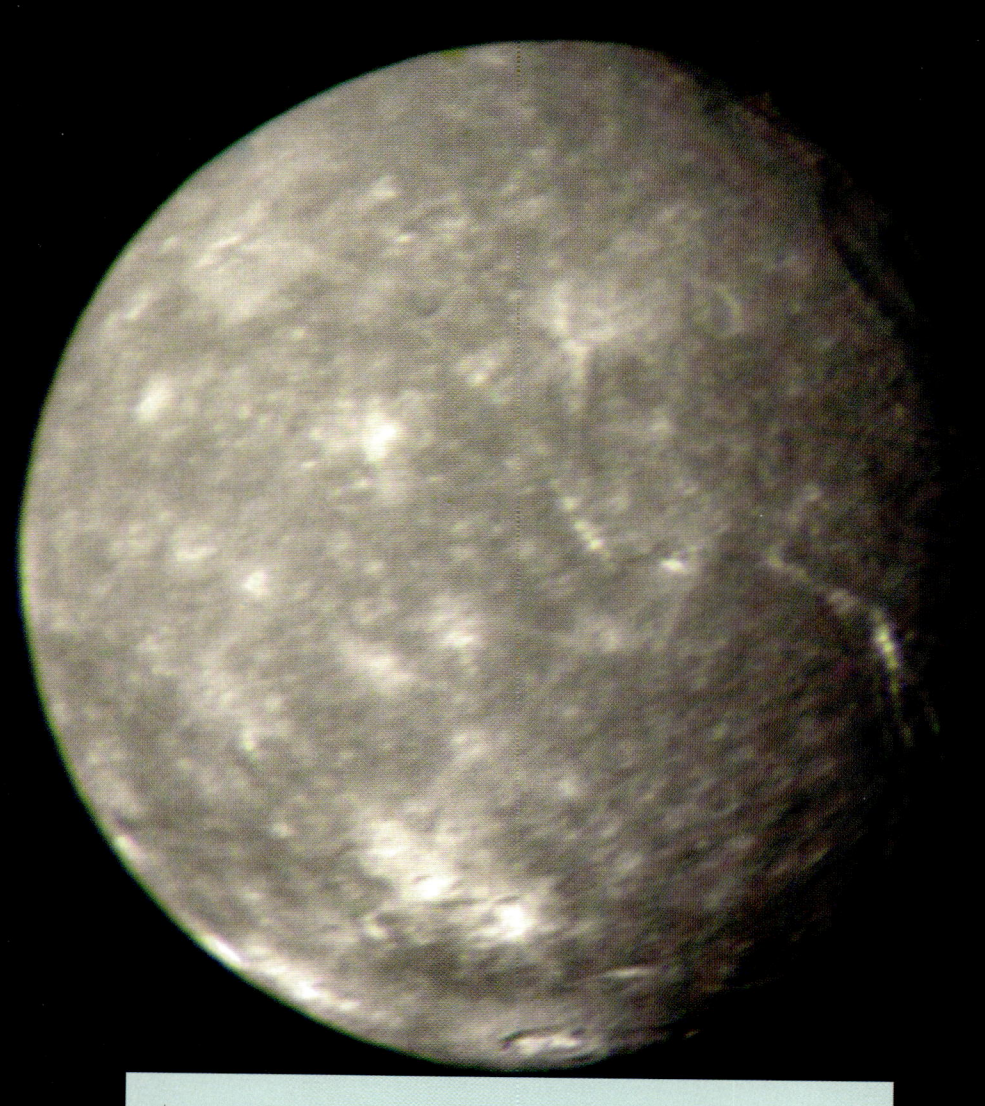

▲ Titania is 272,173 miles (438,000 km) away from Uranus.

The Outer Moons

Uranus has 21 moons, more than any other planet. Most of Uranus's moons are very small. Fifteen of the moons are less than 120 miles (200 km) in diameter. Titania is Uranus's largest moon. It is about 980 miles (1,579 km) in diameter.

Like many other moons, Uranus's moons have many craters. The surfaces of most of them appear to be ice and rock. Most of the moons do not have volcanoes or oceans.

Miranda is one of Uranus's larger moons. It is 293 miles (472 km) in diameter. It is 80,782 miles (130,000 km) away from Uranus. Large cliffs, canyons, and grooves cover Miranda's surface. Scientists think that moonquakes made some surface features. A moonquake is a sudden shaking of the outer surface of a moon.

▲ Triton has an atmosphere made mostly of nitrogen gas.

Neptune's Moons

Neptune has eight known moons. It might have more moons that have not yet been discovered. Neptune is so far away that it is hard for astronomers to see.

Most of Neptune's moons are small. Many are less than 260 miles (416 km) in diameter.

Neptune's largest moon is Triton. It is 1,681 miles (2,705 km) in diameter. Triton is about 220,597 miles (355,000 km) away from Neptune.

The surface of Triton is covered with patches of frostlike frozen nitrogen gas. The surface has dark streaks where volcanoes and geysers have erupted dark material. Geysers are holes in the ground through which hot liquids and gas shoot out.

Triton has the lowest measured temperature of all the moons. Its surface is a frosty −392° Fahrenheit (−236° C). It is four times colder than Antarctica in winter. Antarctica is the coldest place on Earth.

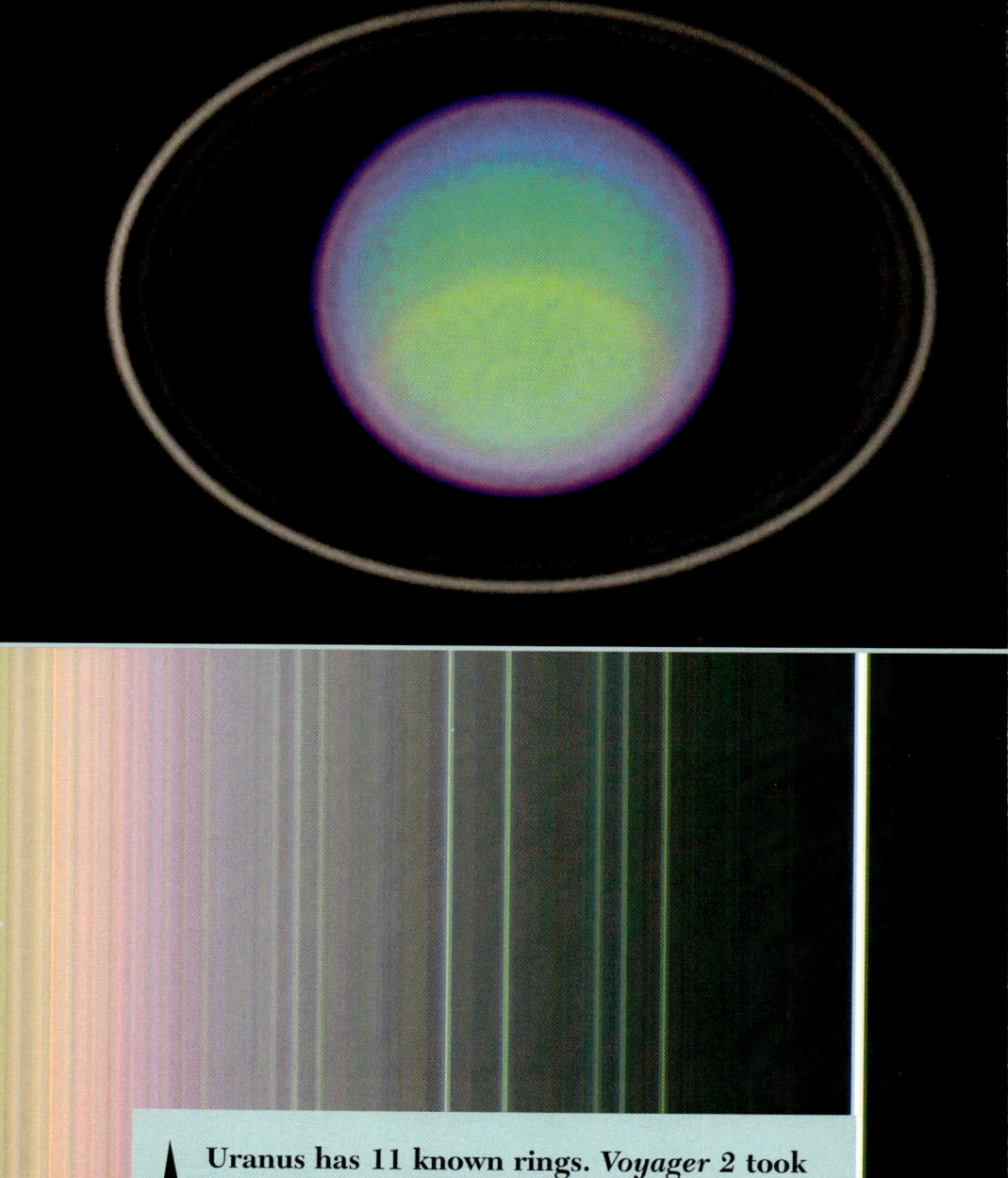

▲ **Uranus has 11 known rings. *Voyager 2* took this close-up picture of the rings (bottom).**

Ring Systems

Both Uranus and Neptune have ring systems. Uranus has 11 known rings. Neptune has four.

The rings of Uranus are very dark. They are made of rock pieces that are only a few feet wide.

The rings around Uranus give the planet a special appearance. Uranus is tilted on its side. The rings make the planet look like a bull's-eye. A person would have to travel near the planet by spacecraft to see the bull's-eye.

The five rings of Neptune look as if they are broken. Parts of the rings are bright, and others are very hard to see. Small pieces of rock and dust make up the rings. The pieces are not spread out evenly. Sections of rings with large clumps of pieces reflect light and look bright. Sections with only a few pieces do not reflect light and look like dark gaps.

More Moons

Astronomers think our solar system might have even more moons. They are hoping to make new discoveries of moons orbiting planets.

Astronomers are sending new space probes into space. The space probes will explore new parts of the solar system. Astronomers will study the information from the probes to look for more moons.

Glossary

asteroid (AS-tuh-roid)—giant space rock that orbits the Sun

astronomer (ah-STRAHN-uh-mur)—scientist who studies objects in space

atmosphere (AT-muhss-fihr)—a layer of gases that surrounds an object in space

crater (KRAY-tur)—bowl-shaped hole left when a meteorite strikes an object in space

maria (muh-REE-ah)—basins full of dark hardened lava

meteorite (MEE-tee-ur-rite)—a space rock that crashes into the surface of another object in space

orbit (OR-bit)—the path an object takes as it travels around another object in space

phase (FAZE)—a stage of the Moon's change in shape as it appears from Earth

ring (RING)—circular band of rock, dust, and ice particles surrounding a planet

solar system (SOH-lur SISS-tuhm)—a star and all the objects that orbit around it

telescope (TEL-uh-skope)—an instrument that makes faraway objects appear clearer and closer

Internet Sites and Addresses

Future Astronauts of America
www.faahomepage.org

Lunar Prospector
http://lunar.arc.nasa.gov/

The Moon
http://www.seds.org/billa/tnp/moon.html

NASA for Kids
kids.msfc.nasa.gov

Planets and Moons
http://wwwflag.wr.usgs.gov/USGSFlag/Space/wall/ wall_txt.html

NASA Headquarters
Washington, DC 20546-0001

The Planetary Society
65 North Catalina Avenue
Pasadena, CA 91106-2301

Index

astronaut, 19
atmosphere, 25, 31, 35

basin, 17

Callisto, 28
Charon, 24, 25
crater, 11, 14, 15, 16, 17, 23, 29, 41

Deimos, 23

Europa, 31

Galileo, 27
geyser, 43
Ganymede, 29, 30, 31

Io, 32-33

Jupiter, 27, 29, 31, 32, 33, 35

maria, 16, 17
Mars, 23
meteorite, 14, 15, 21, 29
Miranda, 41
Moon, 7, 11, 12, 13, 14, 15, 29, 31

Neptune, 27, 43

phases, 13
Phobos, 23
Pluto, 23, 24, 25, 29

Saturn, 27, 35, 38

Titan, 35
Titania, 41
Triton, 43

Uranus, 27, 41

volcano, 33, 41, 43